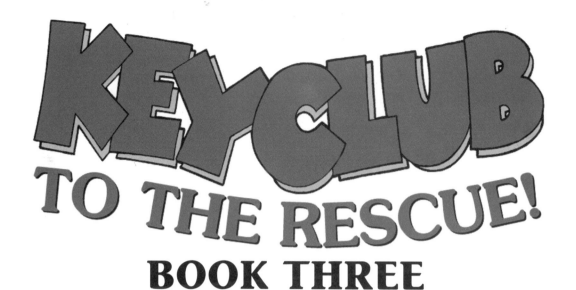

G000095635

BOOK THREE

by Ann Bryant

for all my pupils, past and present

Editor
Louisa Wallace

Cover design by
John Good Holbrook Ltd.

Illustrations by
Paul Selvey, John Good Holbrook Ltd.

Music Setting by
Barnes Music Engraving Ltd.

Published 2001

International MUSIC Publications

© **International Music Publications Ltd.**
Griffin House, 161 Hammersmith Road
London W6 8BS
England

Caring for the Environment
This book has been produced with special regard to the environment. We have insisted on the use of acid-free, neutral-sized paper made from pulps which have not been elemental bleached and have sought assurance that the pulp is farmed from sustainable forests.

About this book...

The pieces in **KEYCLUB TO THE RESCUE BOOK THREE** are designed as reinforcement for **KEYCLUB BOOK THREE**, helping your pupils overcome troublesome patches whilst developing and maintaining sight-reading skills.

As in Books One and Two, all the pieces are short, repetitive and almost entirely free of fingerings, which helps train the pupil to look ahead. In this book the pupil is strongly encouraged to take on the responsibility of choosing the best fingerings throughout the piece including the very first note. There are no dynamics, tempo indications or expression marks, making it easier to concentrate on the notes and each new note appears in the same Keyland area as it does in the tutor book. Word 'snippets' are used to help the student grasp tricky rhythms and also provide added interest. Pupils may feel that they can complete the song themselves!

The piece on page 22, 'Alanis Alarm', introduces the key signature D major, a key which is not specifically covered in the Keyclub tutors. Its inclusion here not only provides a great opportunity for discussion about hand position and keys, it also highlights the connection between scales, key signatures and hand positions. The keys E minor, E major and D minor appear later in this book to afford practice of some common hand positions and note patterns and I have used accidentals rather than key signatures to avoid confusion here.

All the common chord shapes and hand positions for this level are used so the pieces can be mastered easily and the book revisited time and time again as a sight-reading aid – even up to grade 4 level. There is none of the dryness of typical sight-reading guides here, just all the fun of the Keyclub series with a whole wealth of Keyland characters, familiar and new!

Ann Bryant

CONTENTS

Oswald the Owner

Simon the Sausage Sizzling Star

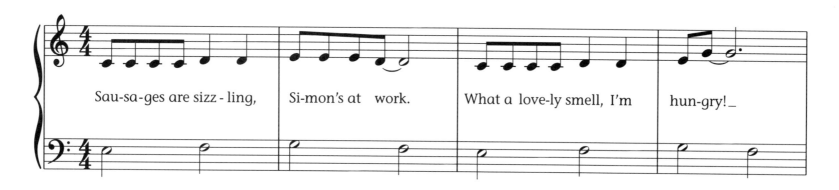

Sau-sa-ges are sizz-ling,   Si-mon's at work.   What a love-ly smell, I'm   hun-gry!_

Ringo the Rope Man

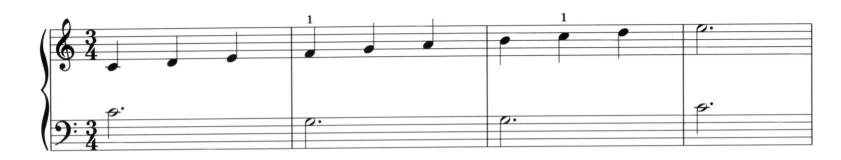

TECHNO-SPECK

Fazz the Faxophonist (on tour)

Play-ing his fax,__ just like a sax, . . .

Mad Malarko Mouse

Dr Wilson the Techno Wizard

Doc-tor Wil-son is a | tech-no wiz-ard, he can | fix a prob-lem while you | watch op-en-mouthed.

Zagger Zoologist

Here he comes, it's Zag-ger Zo-o - lo -gist . . .

Basil Boom the Jungle Drummer

Ba-sil is play-ing on the | Bing Bong Bon - gos . . .

Play R.H. as you want — lots of staccato or not a lot — it's up to you!

Smoothy the Snake
(slithers up the tree of all the notes you know)

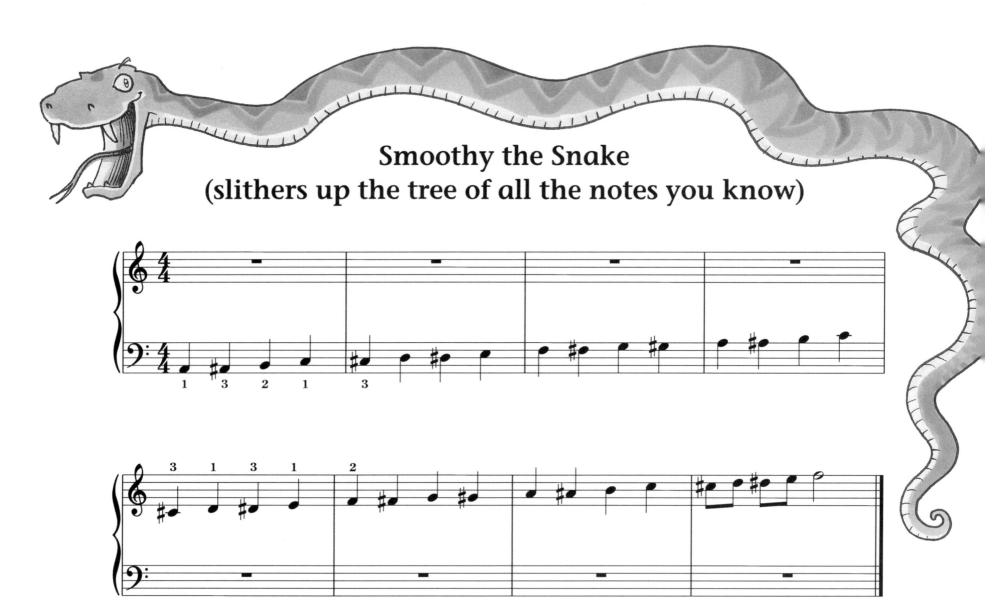

Sokkittoomee Headman

Sok-kit-too-mee Head-man . . .

Elpmeowt the Extraordinary Swinging Cat

Elp - mea-owt's dream - ing of mice___ as he swings.

Fine

D.C. al Fine

Billy the Boot

Bil - ly is the bees knees! Kick-ing __ the ball, he scores a goal!

R.H. High G

The Peking Puppet

(16)

Ting-a-ling-a-ling

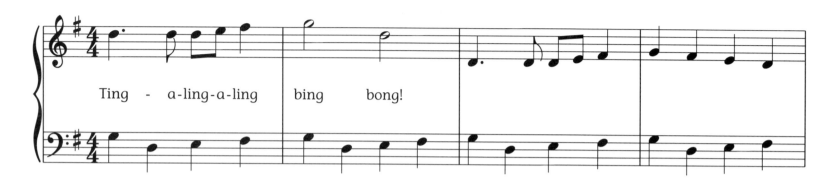

Ting - a-ling-a-ling   bing   bong!

Acrobatic Al

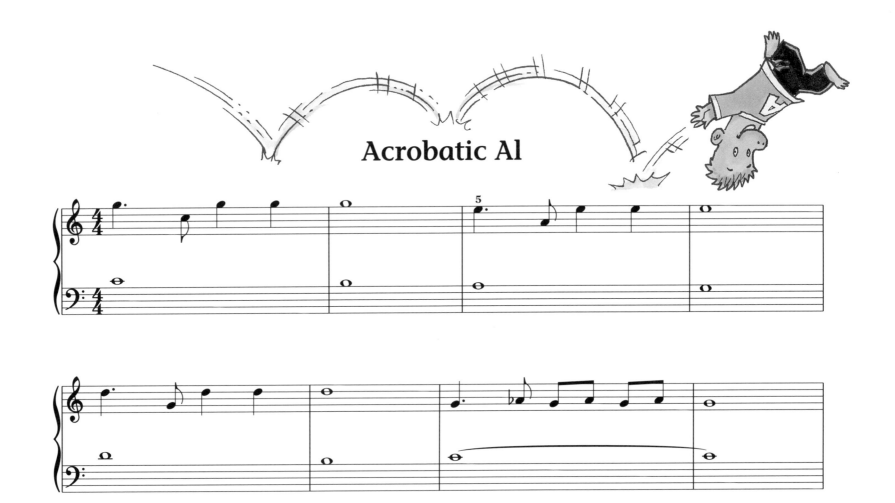

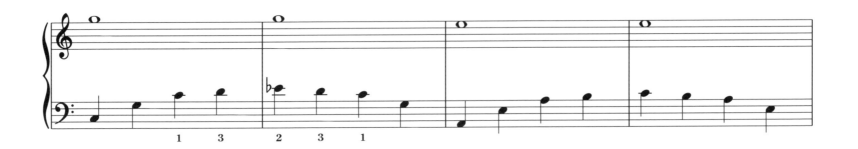

19

Lazy Lullaby

Nambo the Napper

Kevin the Kipper

Alanis Alarm

Your a - larm is set, come on   up you get! It's A - la - nis ring - ing

brrrrrrr!

Here's a brand new key signature! The key is D major. What is the new sharp sign?

22

Walter the Smooth Waltzer

rit.

Jump smoothly!

23

Wayne the Snappy Waltzer

Manya the Mazurka Champ

Cross Patch Craig

Blue Baloo

How d'you do___ Blue Ba - loo?_ You don't look_ ve - ry well.___

5–1 *8va*

Scruffy Scrag Bag

Scruf-fy Scrag Bag . . .

Play L.H. with a gentle bounce!

28

GIANT'S Grange

Gringo the Grim Giant

Look at his shoes, they're | for - ty threes! | Look at his legs, they're | just like trees!

R.H.

Look at his arms, they're | real - ly gross, if you | see Grin-go Giant, don't | get too close.

L.H. over

29

Clive the Clapping Giant

Dave the Dreamy Giant

Say: "One and a two and a . . ." throughout

rit.

There are 5 ways to play this piece!
1) As it is written,
2) With the L.H. an octave lower but R.H. as written,
3) R.H. an octave lower but L.H. as written,
4) Both hands an octave lower,
OR 5) If you **really** want a challenge, swap the hands over so the R.H. plays the tune and the L.H. plays the accompaniment!

Your piece could start like this . . .

etc.

TEPEE TERRITORY

Binka the Minor Brave

Chill the Major Chief and Squattalot his Squaw

Here's that new key signature again! What is it?

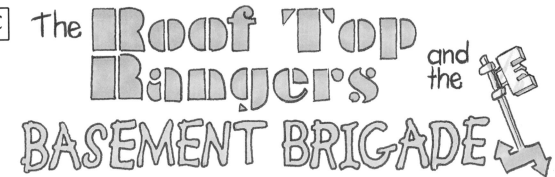

The Roof Top Ringers and the BASEMENT BRIGADE

Barry Bungee

The Keyclub Party

Play L.H. with a gentle bounce!

Printed and bound in Great Britain 4/01

by Ann Bryant

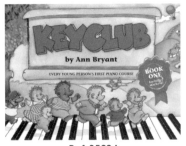

Ref: 3582A

Ref: 3583A

Ref: 3584A

Ref: 5469A

Ref: 5470A

Ref: 5471A

Ref: 5847A

EVERY YOUNG PERSON'S FIRST PIANO COURSE

At last a piano course that's up to date, fun to use and packed with pieces to play, things to do and stickers to stick! The KEYCLUB Course takes place in Keyland – a magical fantasy world of characters and places. KEYCLUB however, is more than just a piano course.
It's a real kids' club that every young person can join!

KEYCLUB More Than Just a Piano Course